TEELINE

ANN DIX

HEINEMANN
EDUCATIONAL

Heinemann Educational Publishers
Halley Court, Jordan Hill, Oxford OX2 8EJ
Part of Harcourt Education
Heinemann is a registered trademark of Harcourt Education Limited

© Text: Ann Dix 1990
Teeline outlines © Teeline Education Ltd, 1990

First published 1990
07
25 24

British Library Cataloguing in Publication Data
Dix, Ann
  Teeline Fast
  1. Teeline
  I. Title
  653.428

  13-digit: ISBN 978 0 435453 52 7

Typeset by Fakenham Photosetting Ltd
Printed and bound in the UK
by Ashford Colour Press Ltd. Gosport, Hants.

Other Teeline titles available
Teeline: Revised Edition by I. C. Hill and Meriel Bowers
Teeline Revised Edition Teacher's Guide by Meriel Bowers
Teeline Shorthand Made Simple by Harry Butler
First Teeline Workbook: Revised Edition by I. C. Hill and Meriel Bowers
Second Teeline Workbook: Revised Edition by I. C. Hill and Meriel Bowers
Teeline Word List by I. C. Hill
Teeline Word Groupings by George Hill
New Teeline Dictation Book edited by George Hill
Teeline Shorthand Dictation Passages by Dorothy Bowyer
Handbook for Teeline Teachers edited by Harry Butler
Medical Teeline by Pat Garner and Pat Clare

Contents

Introduction

Teeline was invented by James Hill.

This course is intended for those who wish to learn Teeline quickly. It is based on James Hill's original order of presentation with emphasis on simplicity and a light learning load.

The book is designed for short courses of all kinds, either in the classroom or for self-study. The instructions are necessary for those working alone, but are not intended to replace the teacher's advice.

It is recommended that students work quickly through the theory and then reinforce their knowledge with revision.

For those studying alone, it is recommended that a minimum of 30 minutes be spent each day on learning the theory and working the exercises. Daily practice is the ideal: 30 minutes daily is more beneficial than 2 hours once a week. The optional exercises have been included for those who wish to spend a little longer on each point of theory and want the challenge of wider vocabulary.

Acknowledgements

I would like to thank the following: Mrs. Mollie Ballad of Oxford College of Further Education for validating the course and making helpful comments and suggestions; Mrs. Peggy Blackhurst for checking the Teeline outlines; Janice Brown of Heinemann for her guidance; and my husband for his encouragement and practical help with checking.

Teeline examinations

A round-the-year speed examinations service, in any shorthand system, is offered to any recognised institution by Teeline Education Ltd., First Floor, 5 Wellfield Road, Cardiff CF2 3NZ (tel: 0222 465398).

1 What is Teeline?

What Is Teeline?

Teeline is a system of fast writing using the letters of the alphabet already familiar to us. The amount of writing is reduced by removing from words all unnecessary letters and by streamlining the letters themselves.

Teeline is based on spelling, although occasionally phonetics are used.

The following simple rules are adopted in order to reduce the amount of writing required for each word:

1 Omission of silent letters:

have becomes *hav*
date becomes *dat*
dumb becomes *dum*

sight becomes *sit*
catch becomes *cach*
hedge becomes *heg*

2 Omission of vowels occurring in the middle of words:

have – hav becomes *hv*
date – dat becomes *dt*
dumb – dum becomes *dm*

sight – sit becomes *st*
catch – cach becomes *cch*
hedge – heg becomes *hg*

3 Omission of one of double letters:

sudden becomes *sdn*
class becomes *cls*
will becomes *wl*

runner becomes *rnr*
unnecessary becomes *uncsry*
accommodate becomes *acmdt*

4 Use of phonetics where helpful, e.g. F for GH and PH when pronounced F as in *enough, telephone.*

5 Retention of vowels at the beginning of words to aid reading:

abt for *about*
evry for *every*

ilnd for *island*
ordnry for *ordinary*

6 Retention of vowels at end of words if they are sounded vowels:

als*o* free iss*ue* radi*o* disc*o* coff*ee*

When you adopt the above rules you are left with skeletons of words. The context will suggest the correct word when you are reading your Teeline notes.

Can you read the following?

Tln is vry esy to lrn.
We shl go to Lndn nxt wk to do sm shpng.
It hs bn a brt and sny da tda.
Pls pt yr mny fr th tcts in th bx.

The Teeline alphabet

The Teeline letters resemble their longhand counterparts and are written in their normal positions when beginning a word, i.e. T above the line; G, J, P, Q through the line. When following other letters, positions are determined by the previous letters.

Vowels have two forms – the full vowel and the indicator.

Vowels are written smaller than consonants.

Most of the letters of the alphabet represent simple commonly used words. These are given on page 6.

Hints for writing

You can learn the alphabet in one attempt or, if you prefer, you can divide it into two or three sections. Whichever method you adopt, read the text and then practise writing the letters, as instructed below.

You will need some lined paper. A spiral shorthand notebook is best as the lines are the correct distance apart. It is a good idea to get into the habit of leaving a left-hand margin on each page for notes and instructions when taking dictation or recording speech.

Rest the book on the table.

Use a biro or pencil for writing. Your notes can follow your own handwriting style, but the important thing to remember is that they must be legible.

Copy the letters of the alphabet in your notebook, saying the letters as you write them. Remember to keep sizes of consonants in proportion and to write vowels smaller than consonants. Follow the direction of the arrows. Repeat this until you feel you know the letters.

Letter	*Teeline letter*	*Notes on use*
A		Full A: used occasionally when it has special significance. Taken from the top of capital A
		Indicator: used in most instances

..../.*...... Indicator: used when it makes a clearer join with other letters
Detailed notes on the uses of the various forms of the vowels appear in Chapter 3

.....b..... ...(6)...... B with the back curved

.....C..... ......C...... Letter C is also used to represent CK, i.e. in lu*ck*

.....d.... ......—...... A short dash written on the line when starting a word or standing alone (the Teeline D does not resemble the longhand D, but corresponds with Teeline T)

.....E..... ...L...... Full E: used before letters Q and P. Taken from bottom of capital E

....l...... Indicator: generally used

....—...... Indicator: used occasionally when it makes a clearer join with other letters

.....f..... Either loop can be used; the direction will be determined by the preceding or following letter. Use for GH and PH

.....g.... ......)...... Derived from the longhand ......g...... It should be written through the line when beginning a word. It is also used for DGE in words such as *ledge*, where the D is silent

.....h.... ......l...... The back of ......h...... It can be written straight or slightly sloped, according to preference

.....i..... Derived from ......i...... and changed into a sharply angled sign with the dot removed. Full I: used before L and V

.... Indicators can be written upwards or downwards according to ease of joining with other letters

.....j..... ......j...... Derived from ......j...... with the dot removed and the tail straightened. Written through the line

.....K...... ..⊀......... Derived from longhand K with the back of the letter
omitted

.....ℓ...... ..(ɢ......... Full L: always written downwards. There is also a short
version which can be written in either direction –
whichever is convenient. Use downward version before
G, M, C and N to make a good join

.....m.... ..⌢....... Derived from .....m..... with curves removed

.....n.... ..⌢....... Derived from .....n......

.....O...... ..O..ᵥ.... Full O is used only in special circumstances. The
indicator is a shallow curve taken from the bottom of the
full O

.....P...... ..↓|...... Derived from ....P...... It is the same size as H but must
be written through the line when beginning words in
order to distinguish it from H

.....q...... ..ᶜ↗...... Derived from the loop which joins Q and U in longhand
.....q.u.... It is written through the line and the sign
stands for Q and U as the two letters always occur
together

.....r...... ..↗/........ Must always be written upwards

.....S.... ......O....... A small circle. It can be written in either direction.
Further comment on this appears in Chapter 2

.....t.... ..⇒....... T is the short horizontal cross-stroke of ......t........ When
standing alone or appearing after a vowel or S at the
beginning of a word, it is written above the line to
distinguish it from D

.....U..... ......U...... Full U is a small narrow version of a printed U. It is
important to keep it narrow to distinguish it from
......ᵥ....... (O indicator). It is used before letters P, R, S, T
and at the end of words

....↓/...... Indicator: it looks exactly like E indicator but they
cannot be confused in context

.....V..... .....V...... No change from the printed or longhand version. It must be written upright to avoid confusion with I

....ω.... ....ﻭ...... Like M, the written form of W is reduced to a single curve. It must be written carefully to avoid confusion with ....ﻭ........ (O indicator)

.....X..... .....X...... No change from the printed or longhand form

.....y..... .....ʯ...... Derived from handwritten Y with the tail removed

.....ʒ.... .....ᵷ...... Derived from .....ʒ........ Use only when Z begins word. When it occurs elsewhere in word, use S

The following additional characters are used to represent letter combinations:

CH   ......ᖲ....... A small C is attached to H

SH   .....ᔆ...... The letter S represents SH and the word *shall*. .....ᔆ...... = *should*

TH   ......٦...... T joined to H
        It also represents *the*

WH   ......ᒐ..... W joined to H and written on the line

Writing Teeline

Remember to keep letters in good proportion to one another.
    Write outlines close together.
    Keep your 'non-writing' hand on the book to steady the paper.
    You can aid the reading of your notes by writing letters above the line when T comes second in a word, and on the line when D comes second in a word. For example:

MT ....   MD ....   WT ....   WD ....

NT ....   ND ....

Reading Teeline

When reading the exercises you will discover that some letters appearing after others could be read as T or D. This is quite in order and you can suggest words for either. For example:

.... *ε̄* .... could be CLD or CLT (*Note*: CD ....⌒.... = *could*.)

This will not cause any problems when reading later from your own notes, because the rest of the sentence (context) will suggest which word is needed.

Exercise 1

Write the Teeline alphabet without reference to the text.

Below are letters of the alphabet joined together. Write down equivalent longhand letters. Can you suggest words for them?

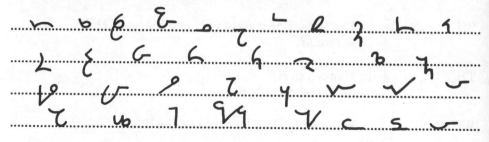

(Key on page 66.)

Special outlines to be learned

Commonly used words are reduced so that there is less to write. They are called 'special outlines'. You should learn the special outlines as they occur in each chapter. The best way to do this is to write them out again and again until you know them.

able ......∧.........   a ....\...........   at ....`........   be ......6........

do ....—........   electric ....ᴌ......   from ......ℓ.........   gentleman/go ?.

he ....l..............   I/eye ..../........   kind ....<............   letter ......*C*..........

me ....⌒............   and ....∩.........   of ....⌄........   equal ......*(/*........

are ..../..............   to ....—............   you ....*U*.........   very ....V.........

we ....⌣............   accident ....X......   your ....Ч........   shall ....S........

the ....7..............

You have now learnt the Teeline alphabet.

You could try writing your own name, and then the names of friends and family. You could even write a sentence from a book, magazine or newspaper. You will be using very basic Teeline, but you will be able to read what you have written.

The following chapters will show you how to streamline and join letters in order to make words (outlines) easier to write at speed.

2 Joining Letters

Joining Letters

Letters are written and read from left to right and top to bottom.

When joining letters together, the second generally begins where the first ends. They are written in one movement, without pause and without lifting the pen from the paper, except where it is necessary to disjoin letters.

Do not try to write too quickly at first. Speed will come with practice. However, avoid the temptation to 'draw' the letters.

Always leave a margin on the left-hand side of your page.

Letters joined together to form words are called 'outlines'. Teeline outlines are read from left to right and from top to bottom.

> Develop good habits now, as these will eventually help you to become a fast writer of Teeline.

Exercise 2

Copy the following letters and write the longhand equivalents on the line below in your notebook. Can you suggest words for them?

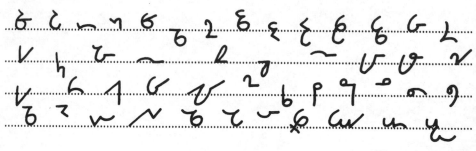

(Key on page 66.)

Letters T and D

T should be written above the line when it stands alone or begins a word, and also when the first letters are ST or vowel plus T:

time .... it .... item .... sit ....

stab .... 　......... still .... 　......... atom .... 　.........

D should be written on the line when it stands alone or begins a word, and also when the first letters are SD or vowel plus D:

dam .... 　......... idol .... 　......... deal .... 　......... said .... 　.........

saddle .... 　......... odd .... 　......... would .... 　.........

Note: .... 　......... = *but* .... 　......... = *bed*, to aid reading back of notes.

Remember also that words beginning W, M, N before T can be written above the line to show T.

The combinations *-ted*, *-det*, *-ded*, etc. are shown by putting one letter above or below the other:

.... *td* .... *dt* .... *dd* .... *tt*.

Note: We keep the first letter in its usual position (i.e. written above the line for T and on the line for D and follow with the next letter, also raising T or lowering D as the case may be).

date .... 　......... tot .... 　......... deed .... 　......... tied .... 　.........

post .... 　......... posted .... 　......... rest .... 　......... rested .... 　.........

state .... 　......... stated .... 　......... wait .... 　......... waited .... 　.........

need .... 　......... needed .... 　.........

Always disjoin T or D after R and the upward form of L to make it easy to read outlines:

read .... 　......... write* .... 　......... halt .... 　......... hold .... 　.........

heart .... 　......... health .... 　.........

Practise writing all the examples just given.

(* Some writers find it helpful to insert letter *i* in *write* to aid reading back from notes.)

Letter F

The direction of writing of the loop will depend on the other letters joined to it. Practise writing the following:

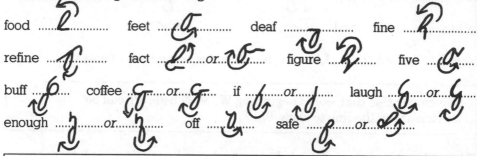

food ...... feet ...... deaf ...... fine ......

refine ...... fact ......*or*...... figure ...... five ......

buff ...... coffee ......*or*...... if ......*or*...... laugh ......*or*......

enough ......*or*...... off ...... safe ......*or*......

Remember to keep your non-writing hand on your notebook to steady it while you are writing.

Take care with sizes of letters. Keep them in good proportion to one another.

Progress check 2.1

Write the following in Teeline:

tap, dip, team, demand, tight, tide, diet, dead, date, dated, rates, heard, pilot, pulled, phone, deafen, tough.

(Key on page 66.)

Punctuation

To indicate a full stop, write a long line upwards, starting below the writing line: ..../........

It is important to include full stops to enable easy and speedy reading of your notes. Other signs are unnecessary, but, if required, use ..../........ for a dash so that it cannot be confused with anything else. Treat hyphenated words as one outline.

......./........ = paragraph. ..../........ underneath an outline = proper name.

Exercise 3

Read the sentences, then copy them, saying the words as you write; now read or write them out using your own Teeline notes.

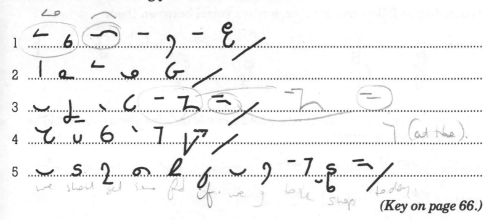

1

2

3

4

5

(Key on page 66.)

Letter S

S is normally written with an anti-clockwise motion to all straight letters in order to keep them straight:

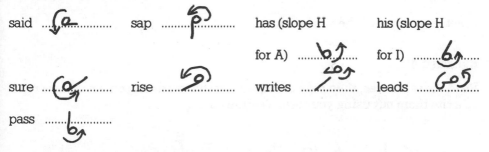

said .... sap .... has (slope H his (slope H

for A) .... for I) ....

sure .... rise .... writes .... leads ....

pass ....

It is always written inside curves:

some .... seems .... case .... lose ....

sugar .... soon ....

If S comes between two straight letters making an angle, it is written outside the angle:

rest .... rasp .... passed .... desire ....

test ....

Where two Ss follow one another, write a vowel between them:

passes ....or..........   rises ....or..........   houses ....or..........

loses ....or..........   classes ....or..........

If S comes between a straight letter and a curve (or vice versa), it should be written inside the curve:

resume ....   waste ....   miser ....   result ....

most ....   must ....

S is written inside the letter B:

bus ....   sob ....   sobs ....

Practise writing all the above examples.

Exercise 4

Read the sentences, then copy them, saying the words as you write; now read or write them out using your own Teeline notes.

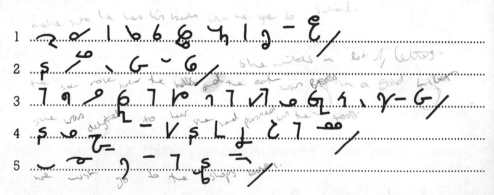

(Key on page 66.)

Letters I and Y

plurals.

Use I instead of Y in the middle and at ends of words. Join it to the previous letter so that it makes a sharp angle:

my .... by/buy .... sorry .... marries ....

many .... money ....

For OY, use Teeline Y to distinguish from Y only:

boy .... toy .... royal .... joy ....

Practise writing the examples.

Letters AY

For words ending -AY, it is sufficient to write A only:

say .... delay .... day .... away ....

stay ....

Special use of I indicator

Disjoin for -ING (written downwards):

being .... reaping .... waiting .... selling ....

making .... staying ....

Soft C

It is sometimes helpful to indicate whether a C occurring in the middle or at the end of a word is a hard-sounding or soft-sounding C, i.e. is pronounced as a *k* or as an *s*:

race .... peace .... dice .... office .... or ....

Progress check 2.2

Write the following in Teeline:

tie, money, hurry, hurries, rely, sky, any, royalty, toys, relay, Ray, writing, holding, sayings, rice, piece, parcel.

(Key on page 67.)

Exercise 5

Read the following sentences, then copy them, saying the words as you write; now read or write them out using your own Teeline notes.

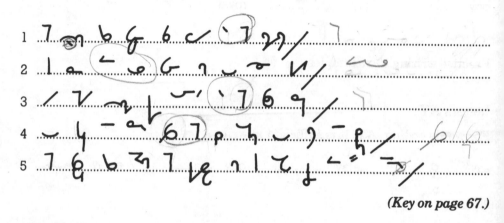

(Key on page 67.)

Letter L

Normally, full L is used, but for facility and clarity use downward short L before the letters C, G, M and N:

luck ......𝓛...........   leg ....ᔑ...........   limit ......ᏉᏏ.......   line ......ᔑ..........

love ......Ᏽᵥ.......   lightly ....ᏵᎫ.....   low ......Ᏽᵤ........

Use upward short L after letters G, H and P to avoid writing too far below the line:

gale ......ᶀ..........   regal ......ᶗ......   hall ......𝖫......   helm ......𝖫........

pulls ......𝆕..........   pillow ......ᛁ......

When upward L is followed by T or D, they must be disjoined to make a clear outline (as for R followed by T and D):

halt ....._r̄_..... hold ....._r̄_..... holds ....._r̄o_..... holding ....._r̄-ı_.....

pilot ....._r̄_..... pulled ....._r̄_.....

Some people like to write upward L after M and N. This is a matter of personal preference.

Practise writing the examples given above.

Writing hint: When T and D are disjoined after each other and after R and upward L, T is written just above the previous letter, and D just below.

Special use of L

P and L with no vowel between them (e.g. *pl*ease, *pl*um) may be represented by writing a letter L through the line if it comes at the beginning of a word, or through a preceding letter if it comes in the middle or at the end of a word. It enables long outlines to be written in a considerably shorter form, thus saving time. It also aids quick transcription.

Note: If a vowel occurs between P and L (e.g. pull, pillow), the P and L must be written.

1 At the beginning of a word, write L through the line to represent PL:

please ...._6_.... plastic ...._6c_.... plenty ...._ʅ_.... plum ...._6_....

plan ...._ʅ_....

2 If a vowel begins the word, position the outline so that L for PL is written through the line. The same applies for SPL:

apple ...._ʒ_.... apply ...._ʒ_.... supple ...._ℓ_.... supply ...._ℓ_....

3 If PL come together in the middle or at the end of a word, write L through the preceding letter:

simple ...✍...   reply ...✍...   employ ...✍...   people* ...✍...or...✍...

(* The short L ...✍... can be used here.)

Exercise 6

Read the sentences, then copy them, saying the words as you write; now read or write them out using your own Teeline notes.

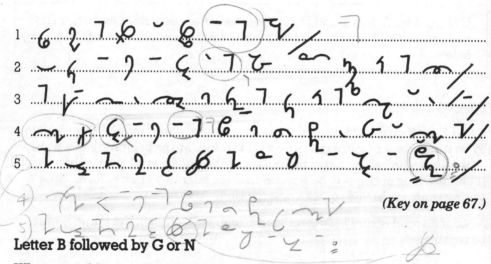

(Key on page 67.)

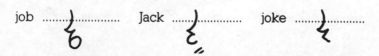

Letter B followed by G or N

Where possible, insert a vowel between B and G or B and N in order to make a smooth, easily written outline:

big ......✍......   bag ......✍......   beg ......✍......   band ......✍......

bend ......✍......   bind ......✍......

Letter J followed by B, C or K

Again, inserting a vowel can improve an outline:

job ......✍......   Jack ......✍......   joke ......✍......

Letter R followed by M

Although these letters join comfortably when written slowly, they can become distorted when written at speed. Thus it is helpful to insert vowels where possible to keep a neat outline that can be read easily:

ram .... rim .... remain ....

Note: If the vowel between R and M is O – as in *room* or *Rome* – write a *backward* O ....:

room .... Rome .... Roman ....

You have covered a number of rules in this chapter which will enable you to write words efficiently. Practise writing all the examples.

Common words

Below are common words to learn and practise writing. Knowledge of these will aid quick writing.

and .... are .... have .... which ....

the .... that .... my .... MAY ....

Note: have – H is sloped to form one-half of V.
   which – both Hs are omitted.

me .... with .... of .... what ....
          (TH omitted)   (H omitted)

very .... be .... I/eye .... there ....

from .... we .... without .... shall ....

at .... to .... you .... if .... or ....

is .... or .... your .... it .... in ....

as .... or .... am .... an .... they ....

no ....𝟚............ this .....(ⵣ)..ᴈ..... these .....(ⵣ).⅂.. those .....⟆........

much ....𝒸........ go ....⌒............
(H omitted)

Words beginning with WH-

For most of the words beginning WH-, we write the H, although it is not
sounded, to make the outline easy to read. Here is a list of the common
words:

who ......ⵣ..... while ......⋎.... where ....⋎.... why ....⟆.... when ......⟋....

However, H is omitted from *what* ....⌣...... and *which* ....𝒸.....

Exercise 7

Read the sentences, then copy them, saying the words as you write; now read
or write them out using your own Teeline notes.

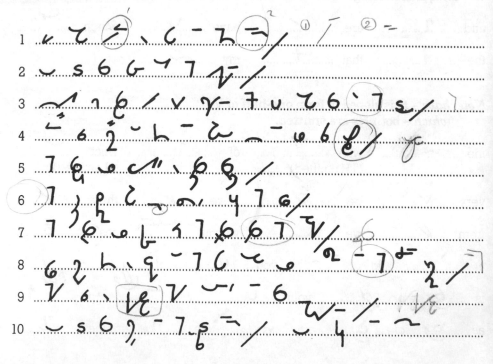

(shorthand symbols)

(Key on page 67.)

Note: Time is saved if small common words are joined so they can be written as one outline. Here are some of those used in the foregoing exercise written as word groupings.

I will	we shall	with the	you will be (omit L)
at the*	it is	in the*	by the
of the*	to the*	there is	to be

(* T omitted from *the* to make a smooth join)

Re-write the exercise using the word groupings.

Some more useful word groupings to help you with Exercise 9

able to   we are*   we have

(* E is written between W and R here to make an easy join.)

Exercise 8

Write the following in Teeline:

1 We had your kind letter today.
2 You are very kind to me.
3 Please will you take the book to the girl.
4 You must bring all your books to school.
5 Do we need lined paper?

(Key on page 67.)

Exercise 9 (optional)

Read and copy the following:

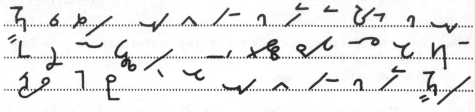

(Key on page 68.)

Reading Teeline

If, when you are reading from printed Teeline or your own notes, you come across an outline that you cannot read, it is helpful to read on ahead and the context will usually suggest the word you need.

If you still cannot find the word, then write down in longhand the letters you have written.

For example:

$$\text{incrs}$$

= *incrs*

This, together with context, will enable you to find the correct word for the outline.

---

3 The Vowels

The Vowels

There are two forms for the vowels: full vowels and indicators.

A – full vowel = ...∧....   A – indicators = ...╲..... and ...╱.....

E – full vowel = ...L....   E – indicators = ...!..... and ...—.....

I – full vowel = ...k....   I – indicators = ...↙... and ...↗...

O – full vowel = ...O.....   O – indicator = ...⌣....

U – full vowel = ...U....   U – indicator = ...❙....

Letter A

The downward form of indicator is normally used:

a ....╲............   about ......б.....   add ......⌣......   all ......C......

am ....⌣....   as ......б......   almost ......б......

The upward form of indicator is used before letters V, W and X to make clear joins:

aviary ....∨╱....   away ....⌃⌃....   axe ....✗....

Special use of full A to indicate AR at the beginning of words. R is omitted and the following consonant is written through or tucked inside A:

art ....A....   article ....Aℰ....   argue ....A⌒....   army ....A⌒....

arrive ....A⌄....

Note: arise = ..A⌐....   arrest = ...A⌐....   area = ..A⌐.. ⁄⁄∧

Full A is sometimes preferred at the end of a word to make a clear outline:

hay ......h......   dismay ...⌒⌒...   pay ......h......

but

way ....🙰.......... display ...�ိ...... say ....🙚..............

Progress check 3.1

Write outlines for the following words:

across, admit, age, again, all, aim, assume, answer, always, artist, arrival, arrived, await, appear, say, may, as, ask.

(Key on page 68.)

Letter E

The E indicator is normally used:

eat   ⌐   ....   estate   ♂⁻   ....   educate ....↳........   emerge ....⌒⌒⌒

tea   ⌐   ....   see ....ρ...........

Note: The other form is occasionally useful for making a clear join:

knee ......⌒....... pea ....∟........... employee .⌒...

Full E is used before the letters Q and P to make a clear join:

equip ......⅄⌐...... equate ....⅄𝖿...... episode ......⌐......

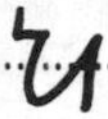

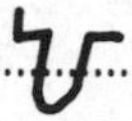

E followed by V is written as ✓́

ever  ......✓́........ every .....✓́...

Progress check 3.2

Write outlines for the following words:

egg, edge, eager, eagerly, elm, energy, else, enough, edit, episodes, equips, easy.

(Key on page 68.)

Exercise 10

Read the sentences, then copy them, saying the words as you write; now read or write them out using your own Teeline notes.

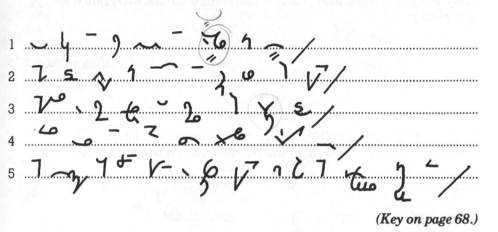

(Key on page 68.)

Letter I

The downward form of I is normally used:

it ......⌐......   is ......6......or......d......   if ......∮......or......∮......

in ......↑......   item ......⌣......   idol ......ℓ......   irate ......V......

lie ......G......

Indicator I is used for Y at the end of words. Make an angle for clear outlines:

apply ......ℓ......   my ......∿......   marry ......∿......   lovely ......ϛ......

carry ......ϭ......   money ......∿......

Full I is used before L and V for a clear outline:

ill ......ℓ......   island ......ℏ......   illuminate ......ℏ......   Ivor ......ɯ......

Progress check 3.3

Write outlines for the following words:

ideal, imagine, items, Italy, Italian, ivory, indulge, tie, sorry, silly, many, sky, plenty.

(Key on page 68.)

Letter O

Indicator O must be small to distinguish it from W. (... ⌣ .... =O, ... ⌣ .... = W.) It is used in all words, except those beginning OR-.

odd	old	open	opinion
offer	ago	also	

There is a special use of full O to indicate OR- at the beginning of words. R is omitted and the following letter is written through the O .

| ordeal | organise | origin | orthodox |

> *Note:* The word *or* is a full O with a reduced R written across it in one movement (i.e. without taking the pen off the paper):

Special blend of O and N

Remove the curved part of N to make an easy join. It must not look like Y.

...⌐.. becomes ...⌐..   ..⌐.. = on   ..⌐.. = only

(*only* . ⌐... can be further reduced to . ⌐..)

Progress check 3.4

Write outlines for the following words:

Olive, over, oak, into, ox, ogre, onto, ornate, operate, original.

(Key on page 68.)

Letter U

The indicator is generally used:

ugly .... umpire .... unless .... unit ....

unsettle .... untie ....

Full U is used before the letters P, S and T to make clear joins:

up .... us/use .... utmost .... utilise ....

upsurge ....

Full U is used at the end of words when it is heavily sounded:

clue .... revue .... sue ....

Special use of Full U to indicate UR at the beginning of words. R is omitted and the following letter is written through or tucked inside U:

urge .... urn .... urban .... Europe ....

Progress check 3.5

Write outlines for the following words:

upon, unite, united, until, ultimate, umbrella, upset, ugliness, issue, urgent, European.

(Key on page 69.)

Exercise 11

Read the sentences, then copy them saying the words as you write; now read
or write them out, using your own Teeline notes.

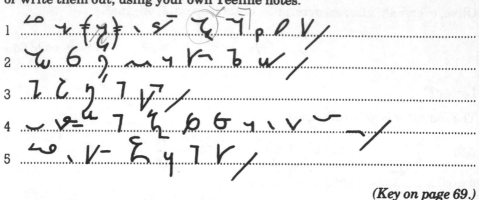

(Key on page 69.)

Representing double vowels

When double vowels begin a word, use either the first vowel only or the one
that has the most dominant sound:

autumn ....   August ....   aimless ....   oath ....

aisle ....   eager ....

When double vowels end a word, write the one which has the most dominant
sound:

blue ....   idea ....   radio ....   video ....

via ....   media ....

Use of vowel indicators as word endings

Disjoined I was mentioned in Chapter 2 as a useful way of representing
-ING. This principle can be applied to the other vowel indicators.

Disjoined A = -ANG   bang = ...   hang = ...

gang = ...   rang = ...   sang = ...

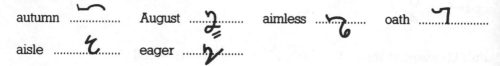

Disjoined E = -ENG (rarely used)

Disjoined I = -ING ring = .../''...   spring = ...ℓ/''..   sing = ...O/....

                 wing = ..◡/... thing = ...]/...

Disjoined O = -ONG wrong = ../◡...   song = ...O◡...   long = ...C◡..

Disjoined U = -UNG lung = ...C'.. rung = ../'...   sung = ...O'...

               sprung = ..ℓ/'...

Other letters can be added to disjoined indicators:

bangs ....6ᴠ.. banged ......6ᴠ.ᵣ rings .../6.... wronged ../◡... lungs .....Cᴠ..

Combinations of indicators can be used:

banging .....6ᴠ/. hanging .....\ᴠ/.... singing ......O//.... longing ....C◡/..

springing ..ℓ////

Note: Special outlines where -ING stands for -THING:

anything ....◝ᴠ/.... nothing ....ʊ/..... something ..O◡/.

This principle can also be extended. Disjoin vowel indicator and add letter C to represent endings -ANK, -INK, -ONK, -UNK:

bank ....6ᴄ....... tank ....−ᴄ......... thank ....]ᴄ...... think ......]ᴄ.........

plonk ....Cᴄ........ junk ......)ᴄ.............

banks ......6ᴄ..... banked ....6ᴄ....

banking ....6ᴄ,.. thinks ....]ᴄ..... thinking ....]ᴄ,.. thanked ...]ᴄ....

Exercise 12

Read the sentences, then copy them, saying the words as you write; now read
or write them out using your own Teeline notes.

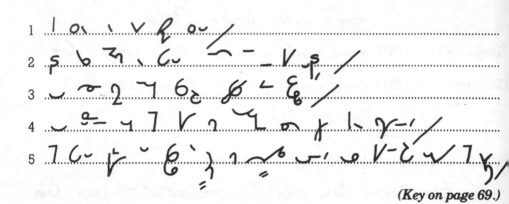

(Key on page 69.)

Word groupings

Time can be saved, and thus speed of writing increased, by joining groups of
words together. Simple common words can be written together. For example:

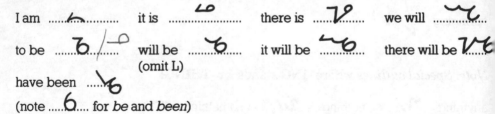

It is also helpful to join *the* to the previous outline. Sometimes it is necessary
to write TH for *the* to make a good join, but in many cases the T can be
omitted. For example:

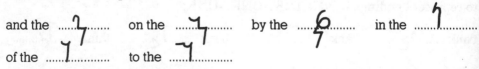

Groups will be used in the subsequent exercises. Those not yet learnt will be
given at the beginning of the exercises so that you can familiarise yourself
with them.

Special outlines to be learned:

number ....2......   representative ....1......

Distinguishing outlines (outlines that must be written in a special way so as not to be confused with similar words):

no ....2......   know ....2...2..   knew/new ..2...

noon ...2...2.   nine ....2....(9)

Exercise 13

Word groupings:

to see ....P........   we will be ....6..   number of ......2....   of the ....1......

to have ....ᐯ........

Read, copy and transcribe (read or write back) the following sentences:

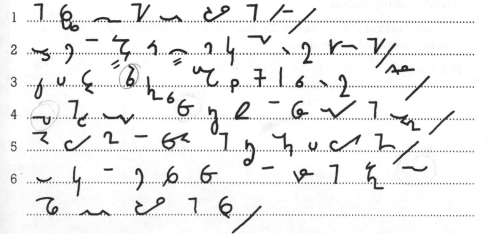

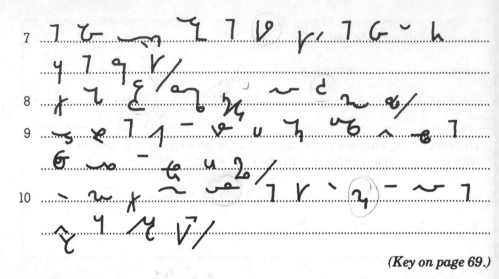

(Key on page 69.)

Exercise 14 (optional)

Write the following in Teeline:

If you arrive at noon we shall have time to eat a light lunch before going on to see the play. I suggest we meet on the corner by the bank. It will be easy to walk from there to the hotel, which has a good bar with a wide choice of food.

(Key on page 69.)

Abbreviating words

As a general rule, if words can be shortened in longhand they can also be shortened in Teeline.

For example: *rep.* for *representative*
co. for *company*
no. for *number*

4 Smoothing the Way!

Blends

Many Teeline letters can be linked quickly and easily by 'blending' them, rather than joining them in their original form.

F blends

F and R become one letter .(......... This may need plenty of practice to achieve a smooth movement of the correct size. Some writers prefer ....
which is perfectly acceptable.

Examples: Practise writing these and all other examples given:

for ....   free ....   first ....   fortitude ....

frail ....   frolic ....

R and F become ....
Example:

rough ....

Special outline:

reference ....

R, F, R are best written as:

refer ....   refresh ....

F and L become ....
Examples:

fly ....   flying ....   flow ....   flan ....

beautiful ....   useful ....   peaceful ....   flat ....

rifle .... film ....

F and B become .. ...

Examples:

feeble .... fibre .... fabric ....

F and M become .... Care is needed to ensure this is written the correct size. Some writers prefer to use .. ... *Note:* SM is .. ....

Examples:

fame .... famine .... feminine .... family ....

F and W become .... Some writers find this difficult and prefer to use ...., which is perfectly acceptable.

Example:

few ....

Special outline to be learned:

business ....

Exercise 15

Read, copy and transcribe the following:

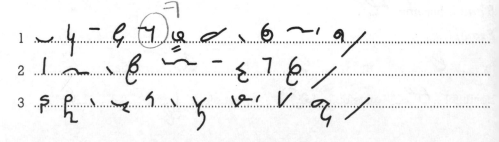

1
2
3

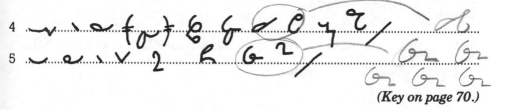

(Key on page 70.)

Check the sizes of your outlines. Are the letters in good proportion to one another?

X blends

Use one stroke of X across preceding or following letter. Omit E when words begin EX-.

Examples:

X-ray .... Rex .... expert .... exhibit ....

excuse .... excel .... exam .... extol ....

tax .... luxury .... mix .... vex ....

wax ....

Note: explain = ... (with L written through the line to distinguish from *excel*).

N blends

N and V become .... with N turned on its side to make do for one side of the V.

Examples:

navy .... novel .... invoice .... never ....

V and N become .... The blend must be curved.

Examples:

van .... 〰 .... vans .... 〰 .... vandal .... 〰 ..... even .... 〰 ....

evening ... 〰 ....

R and N become .. 〰 ..... The blend must be curved.

Examples:

run ...... 〰 ...... random ... 〰 ... burn .... 〰 .... earn ...... 〰 ......

churn ...... 〰 ......

NTH Omit T to make a smoother outline.

Examples:

month ...... 〰 ..... ninth ...... 〰 .... enthuse ...... 〰 ...... in the ...... 〰 ....

N and W. N is written backwards and turned on its side.

Examples:

now ... 〰 .... nowadays ... 〰 .... nowhere ... 〰 .....

W and N. N is tucked inside W.

Examples:

want .... 〰 .... won ...... 〰 .... window ... 〰 ... own ... 〰 ....

owns ... 〰 ....

V blended with H, P

Slope H to include V   have = ... 〰 ..... pave = ... 〰 ....
Slope P to include V.

Practise all these new blends.

Exercise 16

Read, copy and transcribe the following:

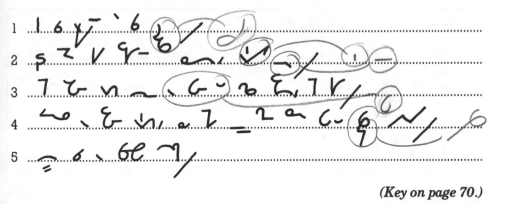

(Key on page 70.)

Lengthening letters L, M, W to add R

LR ..𝒢.... becomes ...𝐿.... or ...𝐿𝐹... or..𝐿𝑅... (but *not* at beginning of word)

MR ..⌢✓.. becomes . ⌢⌢. anywhere in word

WR ..⌣✓.. becomes .⌣⌣.. anywhere in word

It is important to distinguish between sizes of letters. Note the difference in sizes between the letters O, W, WR, and between the letters M and MR:

O .....⌣..   M ....⌢ .
W ....⌣..   MR .⌢⌢.
WR .⌣⌣..

Examples:

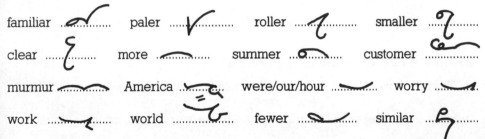

familiar ....   paler ....   roller ....   smaller ....

clear ....   more ....   summer ....   customer ....

murmur ....   America ....   were/our/hour ....   worry ....

work ....   world ....   fewer ....   similar ....

Note: R and R. It is important to make the outline look distinctive:

are = ./.⁊   rare = ./.⁊   ⟋⟍   REAR = ⟋⟍

Special outlines to be learned:

reference ....ℓ....   February ....**6**....   firm/form ..⌒⌒....   next ..✗....

half ....**ʘ**....   profit ....**ʄ**....   expect ....✗....   November ..**V**....

now ....⌒....   public ....**ʟ**....   were/our/hour ..⌣....
Word grouping:
half an hour ...**ᶀ**....

Progress check 4.1

Read the following outlines:

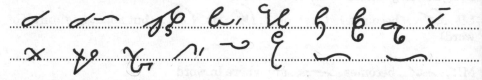

Write the following words in Teeline:

flourish, freeze, female, fowl, reef, vixen, worse, mortgage, navigate, rumours, raining, ruler, paving, exclude, evening, vanish

(Key on page 70.)

CT, CD and K

The letters CT and CD can be written in one movement to make a smoother join, e.g.

cut = .⌐........   could = . ⌐⌐...

K can be written as C in the middle of words, e.g. market = ⌒⌒⌐...

Extended use of R indicating principle

In Chapter 3 you learnt that a letter could be written through or tucked

inside a preceding vowel to indicate the presence of R, i.e. art = ..., organise = ...⟨shorthand⟩..., urgent = ...⟨shorthand⟩.... This principle can be used for the combinations B and R, C and R, G and R, and P and R (e.g. *bread*, *credit*, *great*, *proud*). Its use reduces the length of outlines and is an aid to accurate transcription.

Examples:

bread ...⟨shorthand⟩... break ...⟨shorthand⟩... credit ...⟨shorthand⟩... crave ...⟨shorthand⟩...

great ...⟨shorthand⟩... proud ...⟨shorthand⟩... promise ...⟨shorthand⟩... protect ...⟨shorthand⟩...

prosecute ...⟨shorthand⟩...

Note: Compare the examples above with the following:

board ...⟨shorthand⟩... bark ...⟨shorthand⟩... carve ...⟨shorthand⟩... guard ...⟨shorthand⟩...

period ...⟨shorthand⟩... perms ...⟨shorthand⟩... persecute ...⟨shorthand⟩...

Letter P

Where it is not possible to intersect through P, letters should be written close beside the P to indicate R:

proper ...⟨shorthand⟩... propose ...⟨shorthand⟩... apprehend ...⟨shorthand⟩... prison ...⟨shorthand⟩...

present ...⟨shorthand⟩...

Exercise 17

Special outlines to be learned:

necessary ...⟨shorthand⟩... members ...⟨shorthand⟩... inform ...⟨shorthand⟩... perhaps ...⟨shorthand⟩...

prepare ...⟨shorthand⟩... different ...⟨shorthand⟩... subject ...⟨shorthand⟩... tomorrow ...⟨shorthand⟩...

Read, copy and transcribe the following:

1. ⟨shorthand outlines⟩

(Teeline shorthand outlines — Exercise 17)

(Key on page 70.)

Exercise 18 (optional)

(Teeline shorthand outlines — Exercise 18)

(Key on page 71.)

5 More Short Cuts and Blends

A short cut
-TION

A small N written in T position and separate from the rest of the outline represents -CEAN, -CIAN, -SHION, -SION, -TION.

Examples: Practise writing these:

ration ...../...... fashion ..../...... mention ...../...... election .....

ocean .... deduction ...../...... education .... occasion .....

Other letters can be added to this.

Examples: Practise writing these:

sections .... elections .... suggestions .....

mentioning .... mentioned .... patient .....

efficient .... sufficient ....

Note: In words ending -LY, the L can often be omitted:

occasionally ..... efficiently ..... patiently ..... rationally .....

Exercise 19

Read, copy and transcribe the following:

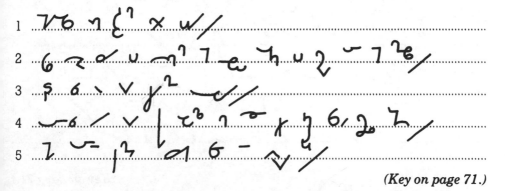

(Key on page 71.)

TR and DR blends

Instead of writing .... for T and R, the R can be moved down and used to

lengthen the T .... D and R can be written in the same way.

Both blends can be used at the beginning, in the middle and at the end of words. They can be used for words where TR or DR come together (i.e. *tree*) or where a vowel comes between, before unnecessary letters have been omitted (i.e. *ter*m). TR and DR should not be joined to one another; follow the rule for

disjoining T and D (i.e. traitor = ... ; trader = ...).

Examples: Practise writing these:

better ....   matter ....   straight ....   strayed ....

travel ....   district ....   military ....   reader ....

writer ....   moderate ....   future ....   picture ....

drive ....   draw ....   during ....   dress ....

Note: The word *order*. This word should be written as .... to
show the first R, but to increase speed of writing it can be
written without taking the pen off the paper, e.g. ....

Exercise 20

Read, copy and transcribe the following:

1. ....

2. ....

3. ....

4. ....

5. ....

(*Key on page 71.*)

> Check your Teeline notes. Are they clear and easy to read? Are the letters in good proportion to one another?

TN and DN blends

TN: ⌐‾‾ . and ..ᒡ.. (.‾‾ᒡ.) become .‾‾ᒡ. ⎫ The top of N is omitted and the
⎬ letter is slightly curved. It should
DN: .⌐. and ..ᒡ.. (⌐ᒡ.) become .⌐ᒡ . ⎭ not look like T and E or D and E.

Both blends can be used anywhere in an outline.

Examples: Practise writing these:

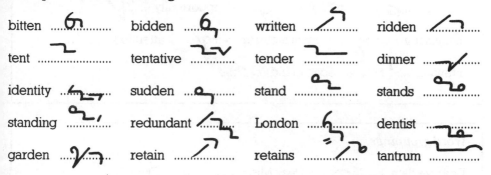

bitten	bidden	written	ridden
tent	tentative	tender	dinner
identity	sudden	stand	stands
standing	redundant	London	dentist
garden	retain	retains	tantrum

Exercise 21 *for next week.*

Read, copy and transcribe the following:

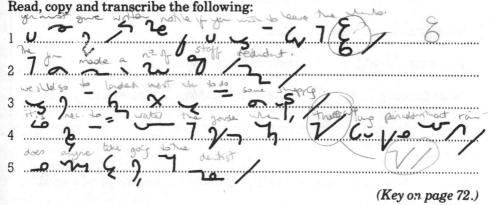

1

2

3

4

5

(Key on page 72.)

TRN and DRN blends

The N blend can be added to TR and DR blends. Both blends can be used standing alone or in the middle or at the end of words.

Examples: Practise writing these:

turn/train .... return .... returns .... returning ....

strain .... stranded .... modern .... children ....

tenderness .... alternative ....

Special outlines to be learned:

extra .... extraordinary .... experience .... city ....

difficult .... difficulty .... opportunity ....

manufacture .... manufacturer .... attention ....

intention .... recommend ....

Word groupings:

Dear Madam .... Dear Miss .... Dear Sir ....

thank you .... thank you for your ....

thank you for your letter ....

I am sorry .... Yours sincerely ....

Yours faithfully .... Yours truly .... as well as ....

THR blend

TR can also be used to represent THR, but *not* at the beginning of a word.

Examples. Practise writing these:

either .... other .... another .... mother ....

smothered ....

but:

threat 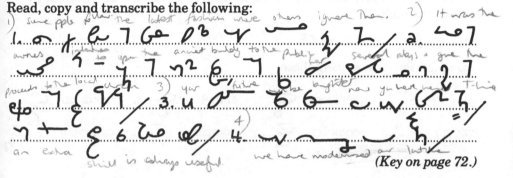 thread ... throw ... there ... there is ...

It is useful in word groupings such as:

that there is ...   if there is ...   that there will be ...

Exercise 22

Read, copy and transcribe the following:

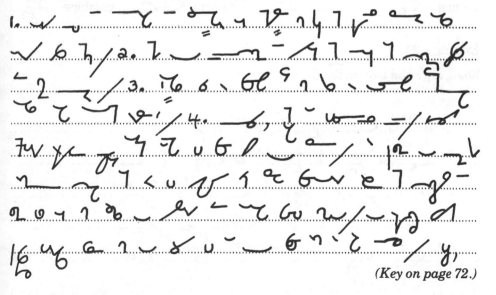

(Key on page 72.)

Exercise 23

Read, copy and transcribe the following:

(Key on page 72.)

6 The C Factor

The C blends

CM blend

When M follows C, write ...⊂..... It should look like a rugby ball with the right-hand side open, and it should be written twice as long as a normal C, but not any higher.

come = ..⊂....; came = ..⊂....

Examples: Practise writing these:

compare ...⊂ᵧ...   compass ...⊂₆......   camel ......⊊......   chemical ...⊊.....

scheme ...⊂......   complex ...⊊ᵪ......   complete ...⊊......   campaign ......⊊ₕ

compensate ...⊊ᵧ......

Note: The following examples contain vowels to make an easier join.

commit ...⊊......   common ...⊂ᵧ...   camera ⊂ᵧᐟ......   combine ...⊊ₚ

Exercise 24

Read, copy and transcribe the following:

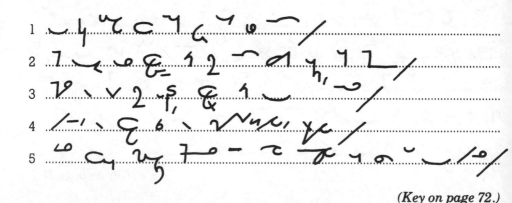

(Key on page 72.)

CN blend

When N follows C, write N backwards, i.e. CN = ... This can also be used for KN.

Examples: Practise writing these:

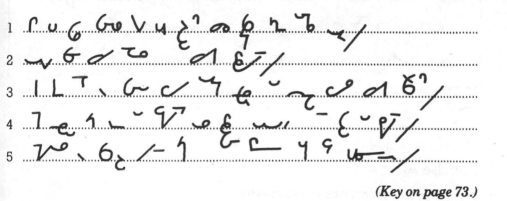

can ....   candidate ....   canary ....   Canada ....

counter/centre/canter ....   cinema ....   concert ....

concern ....   cancel ....   counts ....   concludes ....

consider ....   reconsider ....   taken ....   mistaken ....

cannot ....

Exercise 25

Read, copy and transcribe the following:

1 ....

2 ....

3 ....

4 ....

5 ....

(Key on page 73.)

CNV blend

When V follows CN, slope the CN into the V: ......

Examples. Practise writing these:

converse ....   convert ....   convent ....   convex ....

convict ....

Word ending -NCE

To make a clearer outline that is also easier to write, disjoin C (omitting N) for -NCE.

Examples: Practise writing these:

announce ...🜸c.. announces ...🜸6 announcer 🜸c✓ fence ...𝓁c......

fencing ...𝓁c/... fenced ...𝓁c...... appearance ...𝓎c... since ...o.c...

science ...𝓅c........ once .....⌄c.......

Special outlines to be learned:

council ....ſ....... county council ...ſſ..... difference ....7c..... income ⌇......

communication ⊊ʔ..... convenient ...⌄..... convenience ⌄c....

inconvenient ...⌄......... inconvenience .....⌄c... particular ...ⱴᵗ...

particularly ...ⱴᵗ... develop ...⌐y..... technical ...ⱬ.....

recent ...𝓮..... company ...c⌐..... organisation ...g.ʔ....

Exercise 26

Read, copy and transcribe the following:

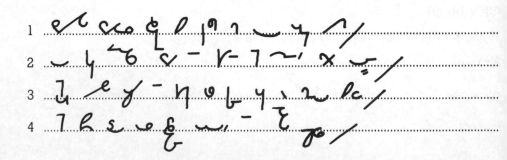

5

(Key on page 73.)

Exercise 27 (optional)

Read, copy and transcribe the following:

1.

2.

3.

4.

5.

6.

7.

8.

9.

10.

11.

12.

(Key on page 73.)

7 Word Beginnings

Word Beginnings

Under-: Write the letters UDR (omit N). They can be joined or disjoined according to which letters follow them.

Examples: Practise writing these:

understand .... understand .... undergo .... undertake ....

undermine ....

Self-: Write the letters SL. They can be joined or disjoined, whichever is convenient.

Examples: Practise writing these:

selfish .... self-taught .... self-defence ....

Trans-: Write the letters TRS (omit N). The S is normally written on top, but needs to be written underneath when followed by M.

Examples: Practise writing these:

transport .... transfer .... transistor ....

transmit ....

Auto-: Write a full A in T position.

Examples: Practise writing these:

automatic .... automaton .... autocrat .... autocue ....

autopsy ....

Progress check 7.1

Write the following in Teeline:

underhand, underline, underpass, undertone, underway, selfless, self-denial, self-control, transparent, transaction, transform, translating.

(Key on page 74.)

Word grouping:

up-to-date ......𝓎......

Special outlines to be learned:

information ...𝕛......   therefore ...𝒥......   general .....𝟤......

generally .....𝟤......

Exercise 28

Read, copy and transcribe the following:

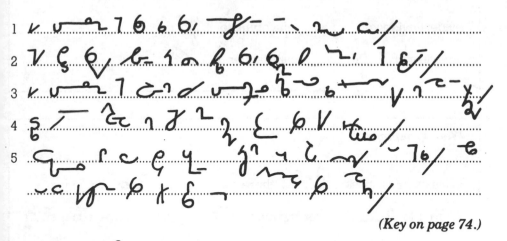

(Key on page 74.)

Super-: Write ......𝓅...... above the rest of the outline.

Examples: Practise writing these:

superman ...𝓅⌐... supervise ...𝓅... supervisor ...𝓅... superhuman ...𝓅...

Over-: Write O indicator disjoined above the rest of the outline.

Examples: Practise writing these:

overcome ....⌣....   overlook ....⌣....   overseas ....⌣....

overbalanced ....⌣....   overtake ....⌣....

Progress check 7.2

Write the following in Teeline:

supernatural, supertanker, superstar, supertax, overbearing, overtime, oversleep.

(Key on page 74.)

Special outlines to be learned:

super ....ρ....   supermarket ....⌢ρ....   maximum ....✗....   account ....c̀....

important ....⊦....   importance ....⊦ c....   recently ....ҁ....

evident/evidence ....∨....   unfortunate ....ȳ....

unfortunately ....ŋ⁷....   circumstances ....c⌀....

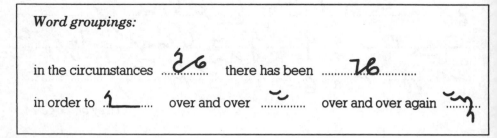

Word groupings:

in the circumstances ....ζ⌀....   there has been ....76....

in order to ...ʅ—....   over and over ....⌣....   over and over again ....⌣....

Exercise 29

Read, copy and transcribe the following:

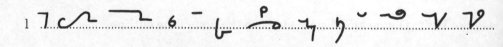

1   ⁊ c ᵣ ⌐ ⌐ 6 — ᖯ ⌢ρ ⊣ ᚺ ⌣ ⌐ง ⋎ Ꮙ

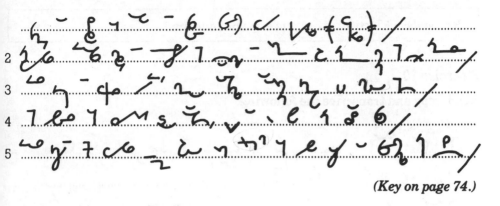

(Key on page 74.)

After: Write full A on the line and joined to the rest of the outline.

Examples: Practise writing these:

afternoon .... afterglow .... aftermath .... aftercare ....

after all ....

Above: Write V disjoined above the rest of the outline.

Examples: Practise writing these:

above-named .... above-mentioned .... above-board ....

over and above ....

Multi-: Write M disjoined above the rest of the outline.

Examples: Practise writing these:

multitude .... multi-storey .... multi-storey car park ....

Progress check 7.3

Write the following in Teeline:

afterthought, above-average, multiply, multi-purpose

(Key on page 74.)

Remember: Electric ..⌐..... is a special outline.

Exercise 30

Read, copy and transcribe the following:

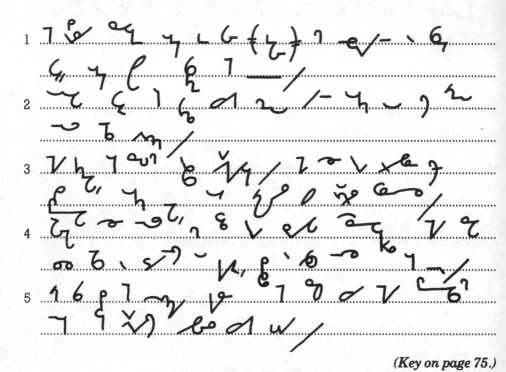

(Key on page 75.)

8 Word Endings

Word Endings

Full vowels as word endings

Disjoin full A for -ABLE, -ABILITY. It should be written close to the first part of the word. Add I for -ABLY.

Examples: Practise writing these:

table .... tables .... capable/capability ....

capably .... available/availability .... enable ....

enables .... enabled .... enabling .... valuable ....

Disjoin full E for -EBLE. Add I for -EBLY.

Examples: Practise writing these:

pebble .... pebbly .... pebbles .... treble ....

rebels ....

Disjoin full I for -IBLE, -IBILITY. Add I for -IBLY.

Examples: Practise writing these:

visible/visibility .... possible/possibility ....

possibly .... sensible .... flexible ....

Disjoin full O for -OBLE, -OBILITY. Add I for -OBLY.

Examples: Practise writing these:

noble/nobility .... wobbly .... double ....

trouble .... troubled ....

Disjoin full U for -UBLE. Add I for -UBLY.

Examples: Practise writing these:

rubble .... bubble .... bubbles .... soluble ....

stubble .... bubbly ....

Exercise 31

Read, copy and transcribe the following:

(Key on page 75.)

Note: The word *possible* in groups – Add PS to outline:

it is possible ....   it will be possible ....
etc.

-OLOGY/-ALOGY: A disjoined O indicator written above end of outline.

Examples: Practise writing these:

biology .... psychology .... zoology .... sociology ....

-OLOGICAL/-ALOGICAL: Add L to indicator.

Examples: Practise writing these:

biological .... psychological .... meteorological ....

-OLOGIST: Add ST to indicator.

Examples: Practise writing these:

biologist ...6... sociologist ...e... meteorologist .... zoologist ...9...

-CIAL/SHL/-TIAL: Disjoin SH close to the rest of the outline.

Examples: Practise writing these:

special ...fs... official ...fs...or...Ys... racial .../s...

marshal ....s. essential ...9.s... especially ...p...

specialist ...fs... officials ...fs...or...Ys...

Progress check 8.1

Write the following in Teeline:

cable, desirable, horrible, edible, desirability, flexibility, astrology, neurologist, zoological, social, Socialist, Socialism

(Key on page 75.)

Special outlines to be learned:

finance ...f... financial ...fs... commercial ...Cs...

Exercise 32

Read, copy and transcribe the following:

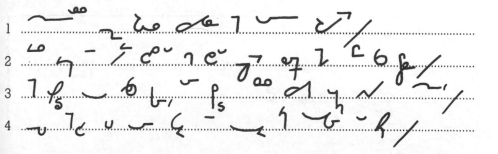

5 ....

(Key on page 75.)

-MENT: A *small* M written in T position disjoined and close to the rest of the word.

Examples: Practise writing these:

payment ....   statement ....   statements ....   experiment ....

Note also:

experimental ....   experimentary ....   fundamentally ....
(omit L)

-WARD/-WIDE/-WOOD/-WORD: A *small* W written just below the rest of the word.

Examples: Practise writing these:

forward/foreword ....   worldwide ....

plywood ....   Goodwood ....   towards ....

-SELF: Write SL only, either upwards or downwards to make a good join.

Examples: Practise writing these:

myself ....   herself ....   himself ....   itself ....

yourself ....

Add S for -SELVES

themselves ....   ourselves ....   yourselves ....

Special outlines to be learned:

arrange ....   arrangements ....   programme ....

include ....   enclose ....

Word groupings:

I think ....[shorthand].... or ....[shorthand]....   as soon as possible ....[shorthand]....

Special note: Take care with the sizes of M and W:

...⌢... = -MENT   ...⌣... = -WORD, etc.
...⌢... = M   ...⌣... = W
...⌢. = MR   .⌣. = WR

Exercise 33

Ready practice

Read, copy and transcribe the following:

1 ...[shorthand]...
2 ...[shorthand]...
3 ...[shorthand]...
4 ...[shorthand]...
5 ...[shorthand]...

(Key on page 76.)

Exercise 34 (optional)

Ready Practice

1 ...[shorthand]...
2 ...[shorthand]...
3 ...[shorthand]...
...[shorthand]...
4 ...[shorthand]...

(shorthand outlines)

5 *(shorthand outlines)*

6 *(shorthand outlines)*

7 *(shorthand outlines)*

8 *(shorthand outlines)*

9 *(shorthand outlines)*

10 *(shorthand outlines)*

(Key on page 76.)

Note: Distinguishing outlines:

century *(outline)*   country *(outline)*   decision *(outline)*   discussion *(outline)*

psychology *(outline)*   sociology *(outline)*

9 Writing Figures

Figures, Dates, Days and Months

Figures

Ordinary figures may be used for numbers provided they are circled so that they cannot be confused with Teeline letters, e.g. ⑦ ⑯ ㊹ ⑥ ⑪. With longer numbers there is no need to circle them, e.g. 499.

Where numbers contain several noughts, it is helpful to increase the speed of writing by using special signs. Noughts take a long time to write.

Hundred – use DR: ..5——. (500)

Thousand – use THS to enclose the figures: ..76.. (76,000)

Hundred thousand – blend DR and THS under the figures: _3_... (300,000).

Million – use M written under the figure: ..2..... (2,000,000)

Hundred million – use a combination of DR and M under the figure: ....8.... (800,000,000)

Thousand million – use THS and M round the figure: ...8... (8,000,000,000)

Pounds (currency)

Use PDS *after* the figure. In shorthand, one must avoid moving to the left as this slows down the rate of writing; therefore it is inefficient to write the £ sign in the usual way.

£16 should be written as . 16....

Per cent

Use Teeline PR ... ... after the figure. This is faster than writing %. 15% should be written as ...15. .

Dates

When writing dates in this century, there is no need to write the 19; therefore 1989 will be rendered as . 89 .... Quote the complete date if referring to another century, e.g. . 1746 ...

Days

Monday = ...～... Tuesday = ... Wednesday = ...～...

Thursday = ... Friday = ... Saturday = ...

Sunday = ...

Months

January* = ...).....or....).... February = ...6.... March = ...

April = ... May = ... June = ...).... July = ...

August = ...).... September = ... October = ...

November = ... December = ...

(* It is essential to distinguish between January and June.)

10 Looking Ahead

Looking Ahead

Hints for writing Teeline

The best way of progressing with your Teeline is to put it to use immediately. Use it for taking notes, making reminders, shopping lists, and taking telephone messages. If you wish to record speeches or take lecture notes, then make use of the simple words and special forms at first, writing some shorthand and some longhand until you have sufficient confidence to write everything in Teeline.

Do not worry too much about making 'correct' outlines. Often there are two or three good ways of writing a word, in which case adopt the one that you find easiest to write and read. For example, the word 'finished' can be written in any of the following ways to suit your own style of writing:

Once you have finished studying the theory you may wish to reconsider the type of paper you use. If you are going to take office dictation or need to take notes and quotes, particularly while following someone who is walking about, then the shorthand notebook is the obvious choice. But for other uses some people find it more satisfactory to use A4 ruled paper. This enables long passages to be taken without the need to turn pages. If you use large paper, make sure you avoid the tendency to write large, widely spaced outlines. You should aim to write outlines close together so that you do not move your hand more than is necessary. This helps the development of speed.

Ruled paper must always be used so that outlines can be positioned correctly, and therefore read easily.

Turn over one corner of the page of your notebook and keep hold of this so that when you reach the end of the page you can flick it over quickly with your 'non-writing' hand. Precious seconds and vital words can be lost by fumbling page turns. Aim for economy of effort.

Revise the theory until you know it thoroughly, as your aim is to write outlines without hesitation. Thorough knowledge of the special forms, so that they come off the end of the pen rapidly, is an enormous aid to increasing speed of writing. Knowledge and use of word groupings also aids speed for some writers; if a word grouping comes readily to mind, then use it

– if it does not, there is no need to worry about not using it.

Read plenty of Teeline – your own and the textbook exercises. The faster you can read, the faster you will be able to write. *Teeline – the shorthand magazine*, published monthly and available on order from newsagents, contains material for secretarial students.

Neatness and legibility are important. Aim to widen your Teeline vocabulary so that you encounter fewer and fewer unfamiliar words. You can put passages from newspapers, magazines, books, etc. into Teeline.

Taking dictation

If you can find someone to read the exercises to you, it will help you to develop the required skills for taking dictation. You will need to develop a particular form of concentration; you cannot let your mind wander for a second. You must learn to listen, select the letters you need from the words you hear, and then write these in Teeline. Obviously, one has to progress slowly at first until this skill is fully developed, so your reader will help you best by reading slowly. Speed will come with practice. If you do not have anyone available to dictate to you then you could hire tapes. Addresses for suppliers can be found in *Teeline* magazine.

It is helpful in the early stages to repeat what you hear to yourself, saying words as you write them. It is not necessary to do this once you have become used to writing from the spoken word.

Daily practice is the secret of success. If you can only spare 15–30 minutes, it is better than nothing at all. Frequent use of your knowledge will ensure success.

Appendix A

Special outlines used in this book

a ....

able ....

accident ....

account ....

and ....

anything ....

are ....

arrange ....

arrangements ....

at ....

attention ....

be ....

business ....

circumstances ....

city ....

commercial ....

communication ....

company ....

convenience ....

convenient ....

council ....

county council ....

develop ....

difference ....

different ....

difficult ....

difficulty ....

do ....

electric ....

enclose ....

equal ....

evidence/evident ....

expect ....

experience ....

extra ....

extraordinary ....

February ....

finance ....

financial ....

firm, form ....

from ....

general ....

generally ....

gentleman/go ....

half ....

have ....

he ....

intelligent
I/eye ....

importance ....

important ....

include	now	something
income	number	subject
inconvenience		super
inconvenient	of	supermarket
inform	opportunity	
information	or	technical
intention	organisation	that
		the
	particular	therefore
kind	particularly	to
	perhaps	
letter	prepare	tomorrow
	profit	
manufacture	programme	unfortunate
manufacturer	public	unfortunately
maximum		
me	recent	very
member	recently	we
members	recommend	were, our, hour
	reference	with
necessary	representative	
nothing		without
November	shall	you

your .... ᴜ ....

Additional special outlines

department .....⌐.......... immediate ......⌐........ telephone ....ƴ..........

frequent ....ᘐ....... immediately ......⌐....... within ....

government ....ʔ.......... object ....ᑫ...............

however ....ᒕ........ subsequent ....ᑫ......

Appendix B

Distinguishing outlines used in this book

century .... country ....

come .... came ....

discussion ...e⁷ decision ...eʰ...

firm ....⌒......... form ......⌒........ farm ...⌒...............

gentleman ...)..... gentlemen ...ʓ...

man ....⌒⌐...... men ......⌒⌐......

many ......⌒⌐.... money ....⌒⌐...

psychology .... sociology .....e....

station .... situation ....

this ....ᄂ......... these ....ᄂ...... those ....ᄂ......

woman ....⌒⌐.. women ....⌒⌐.

Keys to Exercises

Chapter 1

Exercise 1

AM AS BL CLD(T) DS DL ET FD GN HM IN JM KL LD(T) LM LN MK NS OPN PRS QUT RS TL UP VW OVR WT WL YS TH CHRCH WHR CD SHD WD

Chapter 2

Exercise 2

ABT AL AM AN BR DB GD(T) CB CK KL BL LB LD(T) JM HR PN OLD MD FD DF MT QUT QUST NR PR LM RP LR RQUR NT PS SP STP TS SM SG TB TK VW RV WB WL WT BX LYR YM YLW

Progress check 2.1 (page 10)

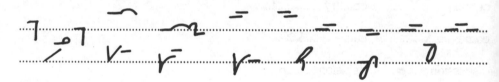

Exercise 3

1 It is time to go to school.
2 He said it was late.
3 We posted a letter to them today.
4 Will you be at the party?
5 We shall get some food if we go to the shops today.

Exercise 4

1 Make sure he has his books when he goes to school.
2 She writes a lot of letters.
3 The sun rose behind the hills and the earth was bathed in a gold light.
4 She was delighted to hear she had passed all the tests.
5 We must go to the shops today.

Progress check 2.2 (page 14)

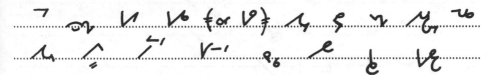

Exercise 5

1 The man has left his car at the garage.
2 He said it was late and we must hurry.
3 Are there many people waiting at the bus stop?
4 We hope to stay by the sea when we go to Spain.
5 The boy has taken the parcel and he will post it today.

Exercise 6

1 Please give the box of books to the teacher.
2 We plan to go to look at the old steam engines in the museum.
3 The pilot made a mistake and landed the plane in the middle of a road.
4 Many people like to go to the sales and some spend a lot of money there.
5 They wished them good luck before they set off to walk to Scotland.

Exercise 7

1 I will write a letter to them today.
2 We shall be late with the report.
3 Mary and Bill are very glad that you will be at the show.
4 It is good of him to allow me to use his office.
5 The boy was carrying a big bag.
6 The judge spent all day summing up the case.
7 The book was put in the box by the teacher.
8 Please give him a copy of the letter which was sent to the estate agent.
9 There is a parcel there waiting to be delivered.
10 We shall be going to the shops today. We hope to meet you there so that we may have tea with you in the cafe.

Exercise 8

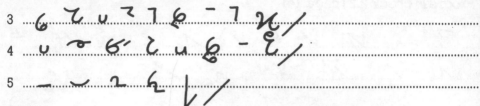

3 ......

4 ......

5 ......

Exercise 9

Teeline is easy. We are able to read and write it already and we have had just two lessons. Doing exercises several times will help to increase the speed at which we are able to read and write Teeline.

Chapter 3

Progress check 3.1 (page 22)

Progress check 3.2 (page 22)

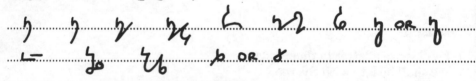

Exercise 10

1 We hope to go away to Wales in May.
2 They should arrive in time to join us at the party.
3 There was a good display of goods at the village show.
4 It is wise to take some exercise every day.
5 The manager of the estate held a big party and all the employees enjoyed it.

Progress check 3.3 (page 24)

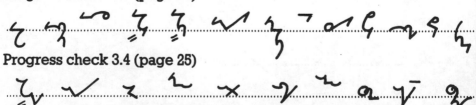

Progress check 3.4 (page 25)

Progress check 3.5 (page 25)

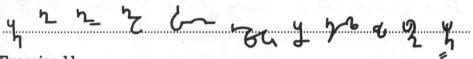

Exercise 11

1 It is only a short walk to the sea from here.
2 Will you be going away on holiday this year?
3 They all enjoyed the party.
4 We visited the island by boat on a very wet day.
5 It was a hard climb up the hill.

Exercise 12

1 He sang a very funny song.
2 She has taken a long time to do her shopping.
3 We must get to the bank before it closes.
4 We stood on the hill and watched some people hang-gliding.
5 The long peal of bells at John and Mary's wedding was heard all over the village.

Exercise 13

1 The boys made their way across the road.
2 We shall go to Italy in May and hope to have a good holiday there.
3 If you look at his paintings you will see that he is a good artist.
4 Do you think we have bought enough food to last over the weekend?
5 Take care not to break the eggs when you carry them.
6 We hope to go by boat to visit the island two miles away across the bay.
7 The old woman watched the horse pulling the load of hay up the steep hill.
8 People who collect stamps eagerly await each new issue.
9 We shall ask the representative to visit you when you will be able to discuss the best ways to display your goods.
10 A number of people met outside the hall at noon to await the arrival of the royal party.

Exercise 14

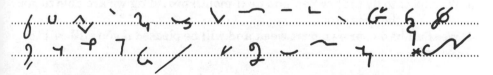

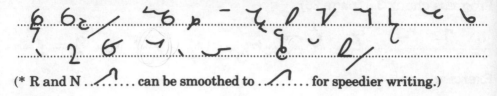

(* R and N .... can be smoothed to .... for speedier writing.)

Chapter 4

Exercise 15

1 We hope to fly to the United States of America for a business meeting soon.
2 He made a feeble attempt to kick the ball.
3 She spent a week in a village visiting her family.
4 We have a few books left for sale on the stall.
5 We saw a very good film last night.

Exercise 16

1 He is expert at his job.
2 She took her child swimming every day.
3 The old van made a lot of noise climbing the hill.
4 It was a cold evening so they did not stay long by the river.
5 May is a beautiful month.

Progress check 4.1 (page 36)

for, freedom, refurbish, flowing or following, cheerful, flag, fables or fabulous, families, exert, next, express, novelty, raining or running, town, scholar, admire, warm or worm

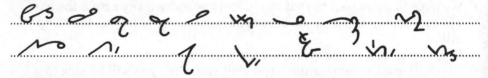

Exercise 17

1 The open-air market is held in the town on Wednesday. It is excellent for fresh foods at low prices.
2 I am sure we shall be able to get to the library within half an hour as we will take a short cut through the park by the river.
3 We expect to fly to New Zealand next month providing we are able to get tickets at the cheap rate.
4 We shall be on our own next week and will be pleased if you will call to see us.

5 It is necessary to study carefully to prepare for exams. Few people enjoy taking them.
6 It is very refreshing to take a shower when you have finished heavy work or exercise.
7 Now that we have learnt most of the blends, our outlines will look neat and will take less time to write.
8 We do not want to go to the park tomorrow if it is raining.
9 Please inform all members of the club that we shall be holding our annual party in February next year.
10 Members of the public will be sent forms to be filled in asking if they want to go to evening talks on different subjects to be held in the town hall.

Exercise 18

Ladies and gentlemen, we have called this meeting to inform you that the club premises need to be redecorated. There are also a few repairs needed to tiles on the floor and to window catches. Our funds are very low at present and we must find a way to raise money to pay for the work. Perhaps members will give thought to the best ways of encouraging people to support us. It will be necessary to hold several events throughout the year. The following have already been suggested: a summer fete to be held in the grounds, a Christmas bazaar to be held in the hall at the end of November and a sports day for all the family. Please let us have any other ideas you may have.

Chapter 5

Exercise 19

1 There will be an election next year.
2 Please make sure you mention the disco when you give out the notices.
3 She is a very efficient worker.
4 Weddings are very happy occasions and most people enjoy being guests at them.
5 They waited patiently for the boat to arrive.

Exercise 20

1 We think it will be better if we go to the beach when it is less crowded.
2 They went straight to the carnival from the office.
3 A lot of buildings were damaged during the storm.
4 The rider did three laps of the track in record time.
5 It was dark and they could not see their way across the field.

Exercise 21

1 You must give written notice if you wish to leave the club.
2 The firm made a number of staff redundant.
3 We shall go to London next week to do some shopping.
4 It is necessary to water the garden when there are long periods without rain.
5 Does anyone like going to the dentist?

Exercise 22

1 Some people follow the latest fashions while others ignore them.
2 It was the owner's intention to open the ancient building to the public for several days and give the proceeds to the local church.
3 Your future will be brighter now you have learnt Teeline. An extra skill is always useful.
4 We have modernised our kitchen.

Exercise 23

1 We are due to travel to Australia on Thursday and hope the pilots' strike will be over by then.
2 They were determined to reach the top of the mountain before it got dark.
3 Wells is a beautiful city and has a wonderful cathedral which is well worth visiting.
4 Dear Sir, Thank you for your letter of yesterday's date. I am sorry that you have experienced difficulty with the tool you bought from our store. At present we do not have another model of the kind you require in stock, but we have asked the manufacturers to send us one and as soon as we receive it we will let you know. We apologise for the problems you have been caused and we assure you of our best attention at all times. Yours faithfully,

Chapter 6

Exercise 24

1 We hope you will come to the play with us tomorrow.
2 The work was completed in good time for the opening of the theatre.
3 There is a very good shopping complex in our town.
4 Riding a camel is a nerve-racking experience.
5 It is common knowledge that there is too much traffic on some of our roads.

Exercise 25

1 Can you please let us have your application forms by the end of this week.
2 We have bought four tickets for the concert.
3 He had taken a lot of care with the display of model cars for the exhibition.
4 The disco in aid of charity was cancelled owing to lack of support.
5 There was a bank raid in the centre of the city yesterday.

Exercise 26

1 Several convicts escaped from prison and were on the run.
2 We hope it will be convenient to hold the meeting next Wednesday.
3 Thank you for your recent offer to help us put up a new fence.
4 The film show was cancelled owing to technical difficulties.
5 The company made a large profit last year.

Exercise 27

1 We shall visit Cambridge for a short holiday in the spring if we can take time off then.
2 We hope our friends can join us for a celebration next month.
3 He was convicted of committing an assault.
4 It was considerate of the speaker to ensure that the meeting did not continue after the stated time. His speech was particularly interesting as it covered many recent advances in the technical field.
5 The candidate was busy canvassing until late on the evening before the election. He had conducted a vigorous campaign.
6 The terms of the contract stipulated that the firm should commence work by the end of the month.
7 The date of the meeting was altered causing great inconvenience to all concerned.
8 The members of the county council agreed that the contract must be drawn up by the end of the week.
9 The fire had got out of control and it took the firemen two hours to put out the flames.
10 The world seems to be a smaller place with modern rapid means of travel and communication.
11 Members of the conference were concerned that the council would not pay sufficient attention to the need for a community centre in the town.
12 It is reported that income tax rates will rise next year.

Chapter 7

Progress check 7.1 (page 48)

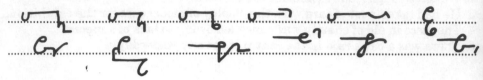

Exercise 28

1 I understand the business is being transferred to a new company.
2 Their selfish behaviour resulted in some fans being banned from attending the concert.
3 I understand the accommodation for undergraduates in this town is extremely poor and much too expensive.
4 She is rather autocratic and therefore not generally liked by her employees.
5 Computers can now supply up-to-date information on all manner of things. Tasks once performed by people can be done automatically by machine.

Progress check 7.2 (page 50)

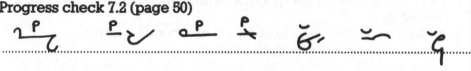

Exercise 29

1 The current trend is to put supermarkets on the edge of towns where there is plenty of space on which to build large car parks.
2 In the circumstances it will be necessary to transfer the money to another account in order to gain the maximum interest.
3 It is important to practise writing new outlines over and over again until you know them.
4 The results of the survey show overwhelming evidence of a fall in overseas business.
5 It was unfortunate that circumstances did not allow an extension of the recent offer of bargains in the supermarket.

Progress check 7.3 (page 51)

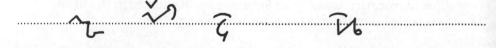

Exercise 30

1 The supervisor switched on the electric light and discovered a body lying on the floor behind the door.
2 We will look at the plans for the new road when we go into town this afternoon.
3 Their handling of the situation has been above reproach. They must have exercised great self-control when dealing with enquiries from over-anxious customers.
4 Although most towns and cities have several multi-storey car parks, there still seems to be a shortage of parking spaces at busy times of the day.
5 In his speech the manager praised the staff for their contribution to the above-average results for the year.

Chapter 8

Exercise 31

1 The building was deserted. They must have left in a hurry as there was a meal on the table.
2 Very few people like walking with bare feet on a pebbly beach.
3 Will it be possible for you to call on us on your way home?
4 This is the time of year when farmers are burning the stubble in the fields.
5 We are grateful for the valuable information you gave us.

Progress check 8.1 (page 55)

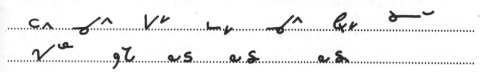

Exercise 32

1 Meteorologists do not always forecast the weather accurately.
2 It is important to write psychology and sociology differently so that they cannot be confused.
3 The officials were busy putting out special seats for the open-air meeting.
4 Do you think you would like to work in the world of finance?
5 Business representatives used to be called commercial travellers.

Exercise 33

1 We are awaiting payment of their account and hope it will arrive soon.
2 He is doing some very interesting experimental work.
3 The car drove very fast towards the bank of the river.
4 We would be pleased if you would let us have the names of those wishing to take part in the games.
5 She had only herself to blame for the accident.

Exercise 34

1 Special arrangements have now been made to hold the social evening in the town hall.
2 The good weather last summer enabled us to enjoy spending time outdoors.
3 The group should include a biologist, a zoologist, a doctor and someone who understands the language to act as interpreter.
4 It is important to write the words decision and discussion in different ways so that they cannot be confused when reading your notes.
5 Speaking for myself I thought the programme was boring.
6 Last night's documentary programme on television showed some of the experimental work done by biologists and meteorologists and the great strides forward that have been made in this century.
7 I think we must soon make a decision on where members wish to go for the summer outings during the coming year.
8 Visibility was poor owing to the fog and the motorist did not see the overhead cable dangling across the road.
9 It would be helpful if you could call at the bank as soon as possible to sign the forms enabling them to transfer the money you have requested them to put into your deposit account.
10 It is essential that all traffic should be banned from Commercial Square once the new shopping centre has been opened there.